Investing in Ethereum

The Essential Guide to Profiting from Cryptocurrencies

By Jeff Reed

© **Copyright 2016 by Jeff Reed. All rights reserved.**

This document is geared towards providing exact and reliable information in regards to the topic and issue covered. The publication is sold with the idea that the publisher is not required to render accounting, officially permitted, or otherwise, qualified services. If advice is necessary, legal or professional, a practiced individual in the profession should be ordered.

- From a Declaration of Principles which was accepted and approved equally by a Committee of the American Bar Association and a Committee of Publishers and Associations.

In no way is it legal to reproduce, duplicate, or transmit any part of this document in either electronic means or in printed format. Recording of this publication is strictly prohibited and any storage of this document is not allowed unless with written permission from the publisher. All rights reserved.

The information provided herein is stated to be truthful and consistent, in that any liability, in terms of inattention or otherwise, by any usage or abuse of any policies, processes, or directions contained within is the solitary and utter responsibility of the recipient reader. Under no circumstances will any legal responsibility or blame be held against the publisher for any reparation, damages, or monetary loss due to the information herein, either directly or indirectly.

Respective authors own all copyrights not held by the publisher.

The information herein is offered for informational purposes solely, and is universal as so. The presentation of the information is without contract or any type of guarantee assurance.

The trademarks that are used are without any consent, and the publication of the trademark is without permission or backing by the trademark owner. All trademarks and brands within this book are for clarifying purposes only and are the owned by the owners themselves, not affiliated with this document.

Table of Contents

Introduction 1

Chapter 1: Ethereum 101 4

Chapter 2: The Double-Edged Sword Of Ethereum 10

Chapter 3: Investing In Ethereum 26

Chapter 4: Smart Contracts 44

Chapter 5: Roadblocks 59

Chapter 6: Tips And Tricks 61

Conclusion 63

Additional Resources 65

Other Books, By Jeff Reed 69

Introduction

Welcome to the world of cryptocurrency. You're curious about investing and have learned about Ethereum or Bitcoin. Perhaps you know the exceptional returns possible for investments in these cryptocurrencies, which have given a massive return on investment (ROI) for those who dared to purchase them at their lows. For example, at one point the Bitcoin (BTC) to US Dollar (USD) or BTC/USD was under $1 while now it currently sits at the $600 range. That is over a *60,000%* increase in any initial investment. Imagine putting $1000 into BTC at its low – you would have $600,000 now! If you weren't aware of those numbers, I might have your attention now.

This book isn't about Bitcoin, but it's impossible to speak about Ethereum without explaining Bitcoin which was the first major "cryptocurrency" used. It's not that old; Bitcoin was born early in the year 2009. It set out to introduce a novel idea in a scholarly article written by the elusive Satoshi Nakamoto. Bitcoin and all digital cryptocurrencies offer an extensive list of benefits to our current currencies such as lower transaction fees compared to traditional online payment mechanisms and banking. Cryptocurrencies are operated by a decentralized authority, unlike government and federally issued currencies. You'll never hold a physical Bitcoin or Ethereum coin in your hand since they do not exist. Rather, the currencies are all held in a virtual field of mathematics of changing balances from private or public "keys" which are synonymous with account numbers.

In this book, I hope to inform you of the reasons to invest in Ethereum and not just because of the potential ROI, but also the benefits of cryptocurrencies in themselves. I will also go over the risks, the obstacles, and major changes in Ethereum. There are over 1,000 cryptocurrencies that currently exist (albeit ~90% are just gimmicks and schemes) so it's important to choose wisely and understand everything you can if you're going to be putting real money into the blockchain. When you're done with this book, you will have both a broader and more detailed understanding of everything Ethereum and beyond.

Chapter 1: Ethereum 101

We define Ethereum as the blockchain platform on which the currency known as Ether is exchanged. The blockchain is open to all for development such that anyone can design programmable functions for executing transactions and trades. That makes Ether and Ethereum a very decentralized system lowering inherent risks and improving the user's functional control over the currency's possibilities.

While Bitcoin was developed in early 2008 and released to the public in 2009, Ethereum came four years later in 2013 and was presented by Vitalik Buterin. It was not until the following year that the infrastructure housing the decentralized blockchain was put into use, and still another year in 2015 until the public blockchain was released. The Russian creator developed the Ether system in Canada while actively involved in further developing Bitcoin. However, it was apparent that benefits could be made to the *concept* of Bitcoin, but would require its own blockchain to provide a complete flexibility in development and creation of applications. Thus, Buterin opted to use a Turing complete programming language. His invention awarded him the World Technology Award for the cryptocurrency's invention. You may be asking what Turing complete means.

Well, you don't need to understand a large amount of math or computer science to be able to comprehend why Turing complete is an advancement for cryptocurrencies. What you do need to know is that Bitcoin, which is operated in a computer language that is **not** Turing complete simply cannot express certain types of actions or contract requirements that would be essential to make projects like Ethereum work.

What had been happening previously was for every specific application that Bitcoin couldn't meet, people would create a new, alternative type of cryptocurrency or altcoin, to produce the results needed for each specific application Bitcoin wasn't able to handle. In one such example, NameCoin had to be developed to register domain names that would be resistant to any type of censorship. This is because Bitcoin couldn't access the type of language needed to get into registering domain names. Another important example is Litecoin which is basically the same as Bitcoin, except it's all open source. Due to the scripting and hashing of Litecoin, however, blocks can be generated at about 1/4th the time compared to Bitcoin, making mining more efficient. If you're interested in all the CCs, definitely research Litecoin.

In a more broad and fundamental approach, Ethereum's foundation is still the Bitcoin blockchain type of technology, but the platform now has a Turing complete programming language built into it. That means the platform can now cross-talk with any type of application you desire, and thus the building of apps (Dapps) and contracts becomes a paramount strength in Ethereum's framework.

Although Ethereum is decentralized, there is a major company and foundation that pilot the paradigm of the platform. Ethereum Switzerland GmbH was the flagship program developer of all things Ethereum at its launch on July 30, 2015.

Additionally, the Ethereum Foundation helps produce and maintain the collective use of Ether coin and is also based in Switzerland. Vitalik Buterin is the lead for the research team at Ethereum Foundation, working alongside others to produce the next vision of Ethereum and its decentralized apps (Dapps).

It only took one year from public release for the value of Ethereum to reach $1 billion USD and begin to give Bitcoin a run for its money. The simple fact is that Ethereum can do a variety of new things that Bitcoin cannot.

Ether and Value

The value token of Ethereum is the Ether or Ether coin. Comparative to Bitcoin, it is exchanged on blockchain in transactions, and carries with it all the benefits of micro transactions (being able to send any fractional value of a single, whole Ether). The Ether currency will be held in your wallet and can be used in the Ethereum network. There is no federally-backed monetary value of Ether or any cryptocurrency which actually brings up an interesting point about monetary value in its most fundamental aspect; *monetary value is completely dependent on people's agreement of it.*

When people speak about how paper money used to be backed by the value of gold, i.e. every dollar had an exact exchange rate for gold, people felt safe. When the dollar transitioned from commodity money (representative of precious metal) to fiat money (government-assigned value *via* federal decree), people became afraid. What did money even mean anymore if gold didn't back it? On further analysis, gold itself has very little intrinsic worth and is actually completely dependent on people's choice of it being an aesthetically pleasing metal! There are properties to gold that make it valuable, but to act as a currency, all people within a given market must agree on the value. Thus, the notion of value between our fiat and commodity currencies used around the globe today is fundamentally no different than assigning a value to cryptocurrencies that ultimately bear no physical form.

There is an obvious fundamental difference between any physical currency and that of Ethereum: you need the internet. Since Ethereum is young and at the time of writing this book barely over a year old, it's acceptance is much more limited than that of the dollar or even Bitcoin. Thus, describing Ethereum as a speculative investment is an understatement. However, as I will explain, making the contracts, to make Ether, should benefit in returns with the more effort you put into it.

Chapter 2: The Double-Edged Sword of Ethereum

If Ethereum were objectively better in every way in comparison to Bitcoin, we would have seen the evolutionary extinction of Bitcoin and the total dominance of Ethereum relatively quickly. Since that is not the case and since both of them are currently in existence simultaneously and in good number, we must evaluate the pros and cons to each. Even though both are built on the same fundamental principle, the blockchain, they have different programs, and each come with benefits and detriments. Let's go over why you would like Ethereum, and then we'll tackle the negatives.

Contracts and the Interface of Ethereum

You can think of contracts in Ethereum as programmable accounts, but also in a legal sense as you would any general contract. They are essentially accounts you can interact with *via* Ether transactions. While contracts in the real world can require attorneys or even judicial figures to be implemented, in the crypto-world this is not the case. This allows for an extremely low cost and barrier for entry into the transaction world. This is due to the Distributed Autonomous Organization (DAO) as the governing body.

Every time you sign your name on a receipt or click the "I understand" checkbox upon purchasing a service, these examples, are the equivalent contracts you will see in Ethereum. However, these contracts in Ethereum can be made by anyone, and anyone can interact with them in an open sandbox like manner (at least in comparison to current transaction 'contracts').

More thoroughly, a smart contract is basically a computer program that has been written in an Ethereum high-level programming language. These languages are primarily Solidity or Serpent. The program is then deployed into a special transaction along with a minimal transaction fee.

When this transaction is executed and deployed, the program is then securely stored in the blockchain and can exist forever.

These types of contracts can enforce or mediate, in a sense, any kind of deal taken between two or more parties. As an example, the recently advanced development of the Internet of Things, we can now design a microprocessor in our car that has the purpose of mediating and enforcing smart contracts. Let's say you have a processor installed in your vehicle. If you intended to sell it, but a specific buyer is unable to pay until a pre-specified (or unspecified!) later date, you can write up your own smart contract such that when a buyer deposits enough Ether into your wallet, the private key will be unlocked for use and he can drive the car. If the contract is not fulfilled, then the engine will only start when you use your working, private key. In the future, contracts can be enforced automatically and specifically by perfectly logical computers and algorithms.

In our current legal system, most contracts are often written in ambiguous, sometimes arbitrary language and words which are subject to our own interpretations. If you and the opposing party differ on interpretations of a certain contract, the process becomes painful and will likely require court cases which will obviously further be evaluated on a subjective basis. Juries and judges are not omnipotent and can make erroneous judgments. Here, with smart contracts, the contract is written in a logical, nearly mathematical way in which interpretation is no longer a problem. With smart contracts, which will be written in a clear and universal programming language, the question of who is correct and who is incorrect is no longer an ordeal as the contract leaves no room for interpretation. Once the contract is deployed into the blockchain, you can trust that the contract is protected and the execution of the contract will take place in a logical, rational, and *mathematical* manner.

Gold, Crowd Sales, And DAOs

As discussed before, people feared when the dollar became unhinged from gold, as they thought it would likely collapse the actual value of the dollar. Of course, this was not the case, as the value of the currency is a psychological, collective agreement only. However, with commodity currency that is backed by a physical asset such as gold, the confidence in value that the consumer or holder has become stronger.

Let's look at an example to illustrate my point. If half the world's population were to move to Mars and start their own currency, everyone would have to agree on how much a single token is worth. This makes very little sense to do until you make it backed by a commodity. Deciding the value of a Mars Token or Moken *requires* you to give it value to a commodity, like gold, water, or oil. You could begin distributing your currency after everyone agreed that a Moken represented one liter of water, or oil, or a kilogram of gold. Over time, the value of a Moken would fluctuate until a global Mars consensus had been reached (generally speaking). However, to actually be a commodity currency, there must exist a central bank that holds enough water (or oil or gold) to exchange every Moken currently on the market for its respective commodity value. When this is the case, the confidence in the value of currency increases, and people worry less about inflation and other monetary issues.

Thus, although it is not required, the initiative to produce a gold-backed cryptocurrency makes sense to promote consumer and user confidence in a currency's value. Using a *contract* through the DAO, a crowd-funded project termed Digix was produced which backs all of the registered Ethereum coins with a value of gold. To show the power of Ethereum's community and crowd-funding efforts, a total that exceeded $5 million USD was funneled to Digix in a relatively short amount of time – completely funded with Ether.

DAOs, Dapps, and Crowd Sales

The use of the DAO crowd sale presented a new distributed app (Dapp) that was quickly and efficiently funded to the total of the $5 million project. The project was completely set up by the board of management and required no legal attorneys or lawyers. If (or when) cryptocurrencies become universally adopted as a major form of currency, the ease of producing large funded projects will become much quicker since the funds are not allocated to any region, the laws and regulations that were once prohibitory for many are now sparse and easily maneuvered around. Therefore, developing ideas in the realm of Ethereum, or other cryptocurrencies, will streamline funding and financing for any project generated.

Ethereum itself is based on a DAO and can theoretically reach zero cost to use in all scenarios because functions are done autonomously via the contracts. In reality, there will always be costs associated with any execution of the smart contracts, so there is always a small drain on all activities done within Ethereum. The point of Ethereum, however, is to minimize these costs considerably in comparison to physical labor, offices, and the infrastructure to run full businesses. Thus, executing a contract in the space of Ethereum is going to be significantly lower than executing the same contract through traditional means.

The Real Benefits of Ethereum

Imagine instead of having employees, housed in skyscrapers, with expendable resources, having to go through massive amounts of transactions and "contracts" done between businesses at their cubicles. Versus a dispersed and distributed peer-to-peer group that largely operates through technology alone and all "nodes" of transactions simply take place on the contracts within a specific business. The costs then become astronomically smaller to execute business and financial functions that most companies have entire departments allocated for today.

The cost in Ethereum is called "gas, " and it is a universally accepted cost for doing any computational work by the Ethereum base. Gas has a constant cost, regardless of the volatility of Ether's value, helping to stabilize the currency and enforce more efficient paths for coding the contracts.

In essence, the real purpose of Ethereum is to create a platform in which methodologies can be built upon to run business transactions and costs much more efficiently than that in use today. For instance, the minimum credit card purchases you can have anywhere (if you're lucky) is 99 cents. That cost is directly attributed to the cost of allocating your account's balance to another account's balance. There is always a net loss of money from any transactions from the consumer to the producer in the case of digital currency transactions because some of that cost is required to go to the corporation that is in charge of moving that money (Visa, Master Card, American Express, etc.). This cost becomes prohibitive for micro transactions and also accumulates linearly with a number of transactions processed. You can think of normal currencies as bulky, weights that can't be divided much lower than 99 cents, or the transaction *itself* becomes a net expense for someone within the transaction.

With Ethereum and other cryptocurrencies, you can imagine that the tokens themselves are infinitely divisible and that the transaction costs can and will become negligible in comparison to that of today's standards. Currently it is impossible to pay-per-second for any type of streaming entertainment. If you were to open a transaction or contract to watch only a second of video and subsequently close the transaction, requiring the payment to be executed, and if you were to do this continuously, hundreds or thousands of times, this would cost the video streaming service more money than they would be producing from you because of the transaction costs themselves! This type of issue is averted with cryptocurrencies, as the infinite division is not an issue, and transaction costs become minimized.

With respect to Bitcoin, Ethereum is more intended for the infrastructure of businesses and intelligently designed contracts to execute business needs and financial transactions. It can be thought of as an alternative to the skyscraper filled with cubicles. Its infrastructure was specifically designed with this in mind, as a "black box" in which to operate transactions through. Like Bitcoin, there is little stopping Ethereum from being an alternative currency to fiat and commodity currencies. You can conceivably trade anything using Ethereum, but this is not Ethereum's strength in comparison to other cryptocurrencies (CCs) – they can all do this. It's rather the computing language that allows the smart contracts to exist that makes Ethereum more valuable than BTC (in my opinion).

The smart contracts that are stored within the blockchain of the Ethereum platform are protected by the platform system similar to how a transaction within the Bitcoin blockchain is executed and subsequently protected by the computational power of the entire network. Since Ethereum is decentralized and all of the transactions are verified at each of the computers in the P2P network, there is no single third-party that has enough power to destroy or modify an existing contract.

In essence, the fundamental benefits of investing into Ethereum is the cryptographic nature, it's anonymity, it's universality, it's divisibility, and most specifically, it's coding language which specifically targets it for automated transactions and contracts.

The Drawbacks

We have gone over the positives of Ethereum, and like any investor, you must also know the risks involved. Understanding the entire paradigm of

Ethereum requires you to understand its weak points in addition to its strengths. Ethereum's most obvious weakness is its age. It is a very immature cryptocurrency, and major portions of the infrastructure are still being developed. While Bitcoin has a large market cap, this is largely due to it being the first cryptocurrency and Ethereum is growing quickly.

While Ethereum is meant to drop the need for attorneys, lawyers, and judges from the expenses required to produce contracts and execute transactions, people are still going to be a part of the process. Ethereum itself is built upon human intention and innovation and thus will always rely (and be threatened by) on the human mind and input. If there are major flaws or updates required for the servers, the entire market can be taken down or act erroneously, which would weigh heavily on people's perspective of its resiliency and thus depreciate its market value. This is not unique to Ethereum, but it is probably due to its immature stage of development in comparison to Bitcoin.

If for instance, major banks began to develop contracts within the Ethereum blockchain platform and a major flaw in the design was identified, the network may be taken down, the bank(s) would likely withdraw their funds, and the market cap and market sentiment would depreciate significantly, thus lowering your investment's return. Thus this stage of Ethereum is likely to be volatile, something that can scare the emotional investor, but has an exponential capability to produce massive gains for ROI.

Although not unique to Ethereum, building business models around Ethereum with the goal in mind of minimizing infrastructure costs of your company by removing the office space and cubicle setting can impact workforce efficiency. It is not currently a large trend for bankers to allow the work-from-home paradigm, but it's not impossible for this to occur on a large scale. This will be in the hands of large corporations to weigh the risks and rewards of decentralizing their corporation's contracts and transactions against keeping the business centralized and homogenous in the organization.

As discussed above, to make informed decisions on investing, it is required for you to know both risks and rewards. By focusing solely on the possible rewards, you are very likely to make massive mistakes with your money. Instead, identify the probability of success in every scenario you choose to put an investment in. With Ethereum your investment thesis should be somewhere along the lines of

- A belief that CCs are inherently valuable
- That more people, corporations, and governments will adopt the use of CCs
- That evolutionary-style progress will continue to advance the uses and applications of CCs
- That Ethereum presents a benefit to business models by reducing infrastructure and overhead costs

- That Ethereum has enough security and resilience that it is comparable or better than Bitcoin
- That short-term volatility of market prices is manageable as long as the above five thesis still ring true

Chapter 3: Investing in Ethereum

Now we will speak about my favorite part, the investing. As with any investment, what you are doing is essentially buying something to maintain or increase in value over time and that the stability in value or growth will be greater than stuffing your money in your mattress. Just like Bitcoin, you will exchange your currency for Ethereum which will be produced in your secure wallet. Ethereum is new, and an evolved form of Bitcoin and thus has differences that the new user will not be accustomed to if they have used Bitcoin in the past.

When someone bought their first Ether on January 26th, 2016, they had to pay a just a little over 0.006 BTC for one Ethereum. After just two weeks, this price appreciated in value to the tune of 0.017 BTC as of the second week in February. That's a 300% return in just two few weeks' time making this Ethereum currency look like a very lucrative part of any portfolio.

That initial Ether bubble burst shortly afterward but has continued to grow, as of September 17th, 2016 the price for one Ethereum is 0.0208 BTC, and it remains the second largest CC as far as market capitalization, with Bitcoin in a strong lead. This is an impressive result for an 8-month old CC and with the benefits outlined above; there is clearly a larger market to be captured, and a larger growth to be had in the future.

We need to discuss how Ethereum actually works. That is, how can we possibly make money off of this? What causes the price in Ethereum to rise or fall, and how can we understand this in a way to properly make sound investment choices?

As we stated above, the value of Ethereum is through its contracts. A simple example contract would be one that requests a specific user to sign into a website a certain amount of times. Once that has been completed, the conditions of the contract have been met, the payload will be released, and the transaction will execute with payment into the contract "signer's" account. The payment is sent out autonomously, and either party requires no other action.

Thus you can see the benefits of this. Instead of using PayPal or any other payment system where you would likely have to show proof of visiting the site x number of times, the payer will have to send funds manually. These funds may not even be immediately available due to "settling times" which are finished within a few seconds with Ethereum – but can take days with traditional banks.

In August 2015 the original distribution of the Ether coin commenced. It was the product of a crowd-funding campaign that lasted just over a month and resulted in a staggering $60 million dollars being reached – the largest ever crowd funded project on Earth!

Some of the major ideas that are likely going to be behind the likely rise of Ether prices have to do with overhauling certain industries, making them more efficient as well as opening up more streamlined peer-to-peer options. An excellent example is the stock market.

Currently, in trading within the stock market, there is always at least one middle-man, the market-maker(s) (MM). While MMs provide the market with liquidity, additional middlemen are not required and more often than not, result in excess fees and deficiencies in making the buying and selling of stock quick and painless. Ethereum would be able to replace your broker in this situation, thus removing the sometimes massive fees associated with buying and selling stock. This is only possible through the use of the smart contracts. The MM, with Ethereum, could produce contracts that offer any user with Ether to purchase stock directly from the MM – this is currently an impossibility for most Americans, who are *required* to go through a broker.

The above is an example of how you would be investing (buying stock) *with* Ether, but it is a reason to invest *in* Ether as well. Any benefits that

Ether can produce in comparison to regular currency or BTC will cause demand for this currency to increase, and its value will necessarily increase as well. You should also be aware of all the major projects that are being looked at within the Ethereum community. If any of these projects are massive breakthroughs and would make things more efficient for people or create a new demand for Ethereum, this would be an impetus for you to be investing in Ethereum. We can look at some of these projects that are going on within the Ethereum community now.

Augur is a Dapp and can be likened to an online gambling platform. This Dapp is going to change the way people make bets on certain outcomes in a dramatic fashion based on its design and broadness in capabilities. Some liken Augur will do to the neighborhood bookie what the electric freezer technology did for the old ice delivery man.

The purpose of Augur is simple but powerful. It will allow any Ether holder to wager money on *any* future event of their choosing. If the event doesn't yet exist, anyone can make an event for people to place their bets on. Software built on "wisdom of the crowds" will set the probabilities, collect the Ether bets, and finally, reward the winnings. Because of the ease in which this can be set up, the price for actually running the show is exceptionally smaller than that compared in the average bookie. Only one percent is going to go to the Ether bookie, which is ten times lower than the average today if you go to Vegas.

However, the design of Augur isn't meant to be a Vegas casino. It has no interest in roulette, blackjack, or poker. It's not so much built on "random" probabilities but rather relies on the idea of "wisdom of the crowds." This is exceptional for binary events such as sports betting, political race outcomes, market forecasts, even weather.

What's truly novel about Augur is that it is not going to be controlled by any single person or entity, and it will not operate on any single computer network. All of the currency within the Augur system will be in Bitcoin or Ether (or other types of cryptocurrency), so no central credit cards or major banks are going to be involved. That makes the legality of the system completely up in the air. If the system becomes successful, regulators and bookies will organize to sue and undermine the system. The problem is, there isn't anyone to point the finger at, as the creators, as well as the users, are all decentralized, and in almost all cases, anonymous. Thus it's success will only bring more attention and success to it.

This is a new legal territory, and we will continue to see new legal territories develop with these decentralized networks. The question is if Augur becomes exceptionally successful for betting on the horse race or betting on the Dow Jones a week from now, can anything be done to stop it? The answer is, at the moment, no. If action were to be taken on Ethereum, it would shift the legal power of any government involved, and that is going to take a lot of time, a lot of energy, and a *lot* of resistance. So for at least the next few years, it's likely that Augur will remain up and running, if not indefinitely.

Augur may be destined to become the web's answer to gambling prohibition—it will do to the betting man what the silk road did to the drug user—but you'd never know it from talking to the developers of the system. They aren't a shady bunch at all, working in San Francisco, attending conferences, and have well-built legal representation in the real world while talking openly about what they're producing to any media outlet interested. There's even an infographic movie funded by the group. As you may begin to see, the confidence in the decentralization of these networks, allows the developers to do what they will, and the *use* of such tools in the crypto-world makes it difficult for regulators to write up a document that could put a stop to it.

Around $300,000 of the total $600,000 that was raised by Augur's funding team comes from a man named Joe Costello. Costello is a successful tech entrepreneur, known to be one of Steve Jobs' top picks for the new CEO position of Apple itself. Following the smart money isn't always a dumb idea.

Gambling or casino are terms never used by Joey Krug, a young Pomona college dropout, but also Augur's lead developer. He and the small team of just five employees use the term "prediction market."

Due to Augur being based on the wisdom of the crowd, as bets are moved in and out of each outcome, the odds will appropriately adjust. This is very interesting because not only does it perfectly price the outcome (based on the weight behind each choice), but it also generates a crowd-sourced statistic. There are already groups and programs that use this crowd-sourced mind, such as UNU. UNU used crowd-sourced (what they call swarm intelligence) ideas to predict the superfecta in the Kentucky Derby correctly. This is correctly predicting the first four horses, *in the correct sequence*, to cross the finish line. Another example, InTrade, which was the most frequented prediction-market up until federal regulators shut it down for U.S. customers in 2012. The "swarm-intelligence" seen there beat the pollsters and pundits by correctly predicting the outcome of the 2008 presidential elections in nearly all (48 out of 50) states. Not only would you be investing in possibly the largest prediction market to date, but also the largest crowd-sourced statistics as well.

What Augur ultimately hopes to accomplish with their platform is to make it possible to do a simple Google search and find the probability of any future event, based on all the participants that took place in the poll. Ideally, this would upgrade our world by creating the availability of more informed policy decisions.

But, what will likely be Augur's most profitable aspect is going to be the cost reducing and convenience aspects in which gamblers, betters, and speculative investors place their bets. Augur actually has the potential to make the world safer by taking away market share in the gambling industry from criminals.

Weifund is another example of something taken from the regular internet and brought to CCs and additionally decentralized. You can think of Weifund exactly like Kickstarter, but it supports any type of CC. There will be ways for Weifund to produce token rewards for redemption in some way or another as well. One of the options through Weifund is shares within a project just like investing. You can then trade these shares on the EtherEx exchange.

Colony has a concept that is centered around the idea of a True DAO. A true DAO is a step beyond a decentralized fund, and into a decentralized company or non-profit. Colony is designed and meant to support a variety of Internet Organizations. Colony will allow its contributors to be reimbursed either in CC or with partial ownership of the DAO itself, which will be proportionate to the value of the contribution.

The Colony project has the potential to bring in the biggest organizations, like banks and financial institutions which require hundreds of thousands, if not millions of small transactions every day that go on in the background. These are meant to make sure everything is running correctly and to verify where money is and where it isn't. Colony works to minimize the overhead expenses of this operation by minimizing the transaction costs but also help remove the actual physical requirements that are needed to house the employees who deal with this back-end banking and financing. Additionally, due to its decentralized nature, the concept of "employee" may even diminish, as contracts for certain tasks can be sent out to be done by literally anyone.

Let's take a look at the total money in Ethereum to understand our upside and downside. The bottom line is that if you purchase Ether, and the market cap increases, the return on your investment will increase. The current market cap of Ether is about $1 billion, while Bitcoin is around $10 billion. The simplest scenario is if you were to buy one Ether token today and if the market cap of Ether went up to $10 billion (that of BTC) you would have made a 10X return on your investment.

The market cap of $1 billion for Ether shows that there is a strong interest in it and that the demand is high. It also indicates approximately, the total amount of money inside of Ethereum (but not quite). With a $1 billion market cap, now large projects, such as banking and financial services can become possible, and the confidence in the system is likely to attract larger players. If or when large banks begin to transfer over their requirements for operations into a cryptocurrency market, the value of that market is going to increase exponentially. When a financial entity moves assets into CC, you can have a great deal of confidence that we will start to see a transition from the fiat currencies to cryptocurrencies.

If the price of Ethereum gets too high, the transaction costs will become too great, and dilution (distribution of Ether) will be required to keep the system running smoothly. This would be a negative outcome for any investment into Ethereum. Financial entities would be wary of this and may want to see stability in the market before they begin to get their toes wet. Ironically, if a financial institution were to broadcast that it was moving a significant portion of its operations into the Ethereum platform, that may actually trigger such a high demand for Ethereum that it requires dilution! The volatility that ensues such an event would be large and would cause any investor to feel some heat from fluctuating prices.

With that said, if you were to be a long-term investor in Ethereum, you have to focus on the long-term timeline, with short-term volatility being a necessary even to find traction within the market, and for value to solidify. Thus, if you believe that the demand for Ethereum will be higher in one, two, five, or ten years (your duration in which you plan to hold), then you need not worry about the fluctuations that occur in the interim.

Let's take a look at the actual steps to investing in Ethereum now that we have some of the theory and the future outlined for us. The first step is creating a wallet. The wallet is going to be your home base, where all payments received are sent to, and all payments outgoing are sent out. The easiest wallet for Ether is likely going to be "Ethereum Wallet," who would have guessed? It's a desktop application and can transfer whatever altcoins you receive into your wallet as Ether, which is very convenient.

Next, you'll need "Geth" – this is a command line interface that is essential for programmers that want to build contracts. If you're not good at programming, you may skip this step, but this is where the most income-generating would come from. Etherwall, a program that will build off of Geth is a way of using Geth to interact with the network with an easy to use interface. This is very beneficial for ease of use for sending, receiving, and creating contracts. Additionally, MyEtherWallet is a go-to for storing multiple wallets and runs on Java. You can use MyEtherWallet offline to make "paper" wallets.

Now filling your wallet is done by two ways initially: mining or buying it straight out. Buying Ether has many options, but you'll likely want to use Shapeshift.io. This is a convenient, easy to use site that requires no actual registration to use. The biggest benefit here is that you can switch between the 33 most abundant CCs currently being used. Create your account with Shapeshift and click Bitcoin for deposit box and Ether for receive box. Use your public address for your wallet depending on the method you used above. You'll likely want to make an initial deposit of Bitcoin into the account, but from here on out, it might be wise to start mining for Ether in the Ethereum system.

There are two major ways of doing this. One is to simply use your own devices to mine Ether, or you can rent cloud-processing power to do it for you.

You'll likely want to do the math to make sure this is worth it at the market's current prices, but it's usually around $45 per mh/s.

Genesis Mining is a great choice to start mining Ethereum. It was one of the most socially active Cloud Mining companies in the cryptocurrency community and has a reputation in the field. It has been a major contributor to a lot to the Ethereum promotion process and has actively participated in the bringing the discussion of scaling cryptocurrencies to market leaders. By being open and confident about the success of cryptocurrencies and mining, Genesis Mining has gained an unparalleled degree of trust in the Cloud Mining industry.

To check your balance and send Ether, you'll need to go to your wallet and "View Wallet Details." You're required to submit your private key to access the data within your wallet. It's more or less a password, and should only be known by you. This will allow you to see your public key, balance, and other important information in your account.

Sending Ether is as easy as looking up your wallet details. Just find the button "send transaction" to initiate this. Make sure your wallet has enough funds for any outgoing transaction, of course.

Once you've funded your account, you have officially invested in Ether. You can now speculate on price changes, or you can put the Ether to use by making smart contracts, the heart, and soul of Ethereum.

Chapter 4: Smart Contracts

The essence of what makes a smart contract *smart* is its ability to verify that the conditions set forth *within the contract* are met (or not met). Instead of a contract that is written by humans, and requires humans to interpret the results from the contract, smart contracts (once created and "signed") will automatically fulfill the contract's deal once the action(s) required are submitted. Since the contract is written in logical computer code, there aren't any subjective interpretations and fulfilling the contract triggers the contract's payment.

Smart contracts are capable of real-time data recording and communication through a nodal network. If you write a contract, for instance, that requires someone to watch a video, you could theoretically pay them by the second. With the proper coding in place, you would be able to see how many seconds they have watched as well as the constant flow of payment that they have received. The thing is, you don't *have* to watch it, once written and deployed, the contract will fulfill everything outlined within the code as is possible.

The efficiency of these contracts is absolute and the cost to create them is minimal and reliant on the computational power required (in general, this will be small) the writing party will see a benefit of financial and time efficiency in comparison to the traditional routes. This is where larger players, such as insurance and finance companies will see a decrease in operating and overhead costs, as tasks required get outsourced or are given to employees that do not require a cubicle and infrastructure.

All tasks that require a person to verify if an action has taken place can now be distributed through the network through contracts and delocalized contract fulfillers, so long as the code is written correctly. To reiterate, here are the major reasons smart contracts will exist, and why a business would want to use them:

- They can express business and financial logic as a computer program
- They will represent the logical, triggering of events as messages to the program
- Use digital signatures to prove the identity of who has sent the message
- Everything is contained on blockchain (verified and logged).

Companies that use these smart contracts won't need to worry about liability issues for human errors that take place in nearly all business aspects. There is also less chance of intentional fraudulent activities (barring the issue with anonymity) because no one can lie about what has and hasn't been done. There is a portion of the Ethereum-contract network called Oracle. Oracle has the job of providing the data that is required for every contract to prove its performance while also sending commands and communications to the decentralized systems, contracts, and people where they are needed.

Oracle additionally verifies that everyone in the market and associated with any contracts are actually who they say they are. They must be accessing the contract from a secured point for Oracle to deem them trustworthy and for the data to proceed. There are inbound and outbound oracles that communicate with external applications and systems. They are required for smart contracts to do things such as release payments or to adhere to the details of every contract.

The inbound oracles give the smart contracts the external data that is relevant to the contract so that the contract can deduce what has been done and whether any aspects of the contract have been fulfilled. The outbound oracles communicate with internal command systems and are required for payment dispersal.

When you make and deploy a smart contract, an Oracle will need to be able to communicate in some way with the data enclosed within it which is otherwise not directly accessible to Ethereum.

Only the most important data is going to be passed along from the external systems to the smart contracts that have been written. This is required because, in cryptocurrency, privacy and security are the normal, expected paradigm.

You can control the level of information that the Oracle has access to, such as *context* for the contract, leaving any information that is not paramount to execute the contract, completely inaccessible. This may be important when working on larger networks and with a large accessible population.

The benefits of smart contracts, I hope, at this point are obvious. It should be reasonable to believe that the benefits of these computationally coded contracts will increase dramatically in the future and that Ethereum is the best candidate so far for them to be executed with. This should begin to build a strong thesis for you to be investing (and probably using) Ether, Ethereum, and the smart contracts themselves. Since Ethereum is decentralized, the peer-to-peer nature of the blockchain gives superb verification and resilience. With that said, there are no third parties involved in a contract directly, other than its verification through Oracle and the DOA.

Being able to read the code of a contract will be something required if you are going to be writing or fulfilling contracts. Once you have a handle on the coding language, however, everything will be logical, and you can write efficient programs (the more efficient, the more likely to be fulfilled and the cheaper to make/execute) as well as read them. What should be noted is that once a contract is fulfilled, it's most likely completely solidified as a finished deal. Imagine writing a contract that requires the person accepting to hand you 100 Ether. If they sign that contract, they will pay you 100 Ether, and you will receive it. Depending on the privacy of the contract, that person will have no access to any of your information at all, and no way to dispute any problem. The inverse, of course, is also true, so being able to read logical programming language will be essential for taking on contracts as well as writing them!

As the owner of any contract you write (or buy), you will be required to fill the payment details if the contract is to be fulfilled. How to write your own contract will begin with downloading Solidity, which is a programming language similar to Javascript. Another option would use the programming language that is web based, called Cosmo. Cosmo has a benefit of being able to be sent directly to the network. Accessing the contract requires another program called Ethereum Web3.ja. With either Cosmo or Solidity, you'll still need to follow the same steps outlined below. Without following these steps to completion, you may risk a contract that malfunctions or not be able to upload to the network at all.

Once in the network, your contract can be distributed to all of the necessary application frameworks. This will make it much easier for you if you prefer not to have to go through everything when it comes to actually uploading your contract. There will also be less human error possible when done this way. The framework is there only to guide you; you will still need to have some input and work done for everything to work properly. Thankfully, there are many ways to debug possible errors in contracts and make sure they work properly before uploading them into the network as final projects. You should only deploy perfectly working contracts, or you will risk possibly serious issues, such as paying for an unexecuted, or only partially fulfilled contract!

There are many frameworks to use; some of the most popular are Embark, Truffle, Meteor, and API. You should read some on each to make sure they suit your needs.

Once you have all the programming and frameworks to build your smart contract, the actual steps to creating it are highlighted below. Just remember that each contract will be different based on who is writing it, as well as every person fulfilling a contract may also execute the solution differently.

1. You will need to create an Ethereum node to write the contract on. To do this, you'll download that program touched on earlier called Geth. Geth is an accessibility program for the main interface which Ethereum nodes are implemented within, and Ethereum itself uses. Other programs that are needed will be on the Ethereum website (www.ethereum.org), or they will correctly link you to trusted, required sites. Make sure that the sites are trusted!

2. Once downloading of your application is complete and it launches correctly, you will need to compile a smart contract with the use of Solidity or Cosmo as referenced earlier. These programs will execute your program, or contract, and tell you if it is working properly as you expect it to. No worries if something isn't to your liking, you can always edit your

contract at a later time as long as it has not been deployed.

3. After finishing the contract, you can deploy it. To deploy a contract, you will have to spend Ether to have it "hosted" on Ethereum so that others can access it and sign it. You will also sign the contract to let the network know you are the owner.

4. Now you will obtain a blockchain address and API for your contract. You *can* call your contract back by use of the API, but you will most certainly want to try to work everything out before deploying the contract. Also realize that you could be spending Ether every time you put up or take down your contract, or interact with your contract!

Creating the contract and putting it onto the Ethereum network requires that you test it to make sure it will work as it did in the debugging stage before deploying. Ethereum itself has a basal expectation of all contracts hosted on the network, so you will need to make sure that you fall into those correct assumptions. While being the sole owner of the contract, you are the one who determines the end goals of the contract. However, Ethereum itself will need to look and make sure your logical code is correct and communicable across the network. There are a few steps to make this process easy and irrelevant for future contracts you pursue.

Testing your transaction times is essential because you'll need the network time for verification. If you set the transaction time too low, a savvy "hacker" may be able to swindle more money from your contract than you initially intended by sending hundreds of commands per second. This doesn't give enough time for everything to be verified, and as such will cause the network to lag in response to you submitting payments, which could amount to more than you anticipated for! You should be able to code, into your program, a way to defend against this type of "attack" but to be safe, make sure there is always a delay for sending payments that are at least 10 seconds. This will give enough time for the peer-to-peer network to verify what is going on. You may want to set up a basic "trial" contract to make sure you understand the process as you move forward.

1. Use Solidity to be able to access your Ethereum nodes (contracts). You also need to keep your Python library separated from the virtual environment that you are going to be working in. This ensures that you're not using local environments for network environments, and you're also not placing your contract in a place you didn't intend.

2. You'll need to start with a new client node with your console window. Begin with Truffle or the other framework applications mentioned in the new window and deploy your contract with the "truffle deploy" command. This is a boilerplate contract, and the program is going to automatically detect obvious bugs with this while additionally testing transaction times.

Just remember that 10 seconds is a good amount.

3. Once deployed, it will be beneficial to run a compile in your framework program such that you make sure your contract is accurately compiled to your specification.

If your program is not at risk of potentially being lost, stolen, or draining your account (or any other danger), you can deploy your program onto the Ethereum network to debug there. This is more expensive and riskier, but will most accurately predict if there are issues you need to resolve.

Once the contract is completely debugged and you feel safe, it's time actually to deploy it (finally) to the network.

- In Truffle, you'll specify "truffle init" for a new directory which you can specify.
- Identify your contract to put within the directory.

- Open config/app.json and add your contract to the contracts area that is provided by Truffle.

- Restart your node in a new window and run the command "tesrpc".

- Now you will be ready to run the root directory, verify the contract is on the network in a manner you wish it to be.

Now you can test run using Truffle in the root directory and make sure all tests pass. Once sufficient to your liking, you can add the UI to the Truffle Directory and run Truffle such that the UI is automatically compiled and created by the contract and it can be created in any directory.

Recompiling the contract regularly is a good idea to assure that the application is running correctly and all changes made are reflected within the Truffle program. The App directory is where the boiler points are housed and will help with the UI as well as the distribution for the contract you've written. If access is needed, you have to start the Truffle Watch process and then reopen your root directory in the browser window. Now you'll need to open the developer and do a right click to choose the selection you need to inspect. On this screen, you should add the "window.onload" function so that you can ensure the contract is actually activated when your page loads.

Make sure all your functions are copied over and that any testing assertions are removed, and that output is returned to normal using your console. Here, all you should need to do is load Meteor and create your UI so that it is easily used for interaction between anyone and your contract. The better the UI, the simpler and easier the interaction will be.

Chapter 5: Roadblocks

All new things have a development stage. Knowing what's hindered people in the past will help expedite your learning process and get you into the market quicker. Let's go over some of these roadblocks.

Scalability is an issue that is within the mainstream payment networks because there are about 2000 transactions a second. You will need to change the block size limit so that there are more supportable transactions per second. It is possible at the current stage that if Ethereum were to increase in size dramatically, there is an issue of finite nodes being able to be used.

Some transaction blocks require over half the network hash power to reverse. This is partially due to the high-security needs and could be remedied if reversals cost the initiator a fee.

Stamping is an issue currently as well. Generally, in the blockchain, blocks are made every single day. However, creating blocks more frequently causes the payment systems to become incredibly slow. Thus the network works most efficiently with a specific number of blocks made per day. Additionally, since each user is given a specific time stamp (distributed along a normal curve), and thus no nodes are ever within 20 seconds of each other, thus making communication between nodes purposefully delayed.

There are other roadblocks, but the developers are all working on streamlining every step of the process within Ethereum and smart contracts. Patience is a virtue when waiting for developers to fix problems.

Chapter 6: Tips and Tricks

1. Keep separate wallets. It's not wise to have all your money in one place. You will want to keep the Ether you spend apart from the Ether you make, and the part of the Ether you're saving. Although it is difficult to hack in Ethereum, it's not hard to find flaws in contracts. If you were to mistakenly make it easy for someone to withdraw a lot of funds from your wallet through a contract you made, you'd thank yourself if that wallet had a fraction of your total Ether.

2. Keep your savings in a paper, or offline wallet. Since you won't be using them often, it's just generally safer to keep savings away from online wallets.

3. Protect your privacy as much as you possibly can. Obtaining cryptographic programs such as TrueCrypt are essential to maintaining an anonymous identity and protecting your

information when communicating anywhere on the web.

4. Backup everything and do it often. All the work you do can be lost and if you store anything on your desktop, losing that could mean losing access to your account. Backup everything digitally and physically if possible in different storage forms. Private and public keys should be kept in secure (but safe) places.

5. Do not share any information that you feel uncomfortable sharing. Your public key is ok, but it is just one step closer to being able to access data or Ether from your account, so keep it hidden unless it's required to be given out.

Conclusion

This book is meant to get your toes wet and further your curiosity into the world of Ethereum. It is certainly not all encompassing of everything Ethereum, as you'll also need to learn the specific languages that Ethereum operates on. Make sure you read as much as you can and until you feel absolutely comfortable with CCs, Ethereum, and smart contracts before putting serious amounts of money at risk.

With that, you should have everything you need to enter into the world of cryptocurrencies, transition into Ethereum, start organizing yourself to write contracts and deploying your first smart contract onto the Ethereum platform. You can decide whether generating income by writing contracts that generate goods that you can sell, by buying and selling contracts themselves or fulfilling contracts on your own is how you want to earn your Ether. You may also find that you don't need to withdraw Ether at all, and you end up using it as an alternative to fiat currency. Or, you could simply watch your initial ETH/USD value increase!

Additional Resources

Below are some additional noteworthy resources:

www.Ethereum.org

This is made by the people who started Ethereum and will set you off on everything from the history to the various projects being made currently.

www.Ether.fund

Here you can find nearly every tool you'll ever need to get started with investing in Ethereum and creating smart contracts and expanding the ecosystem. It will compare and contrast different tools for you as well.

www.cryptomining-blog.com

This blog will give you files and information to help improve your ability to navigate the platform that is Ethereum. You can look for troubleshooting and other news within the world of Ether here.

www.cryptomining-blog.com/5325-quick-guide-on-how-to-mine-thereum-on-windows

This is a quick and efficient guide for anyone looking to get into mining Ethereum at an accelerated and acceptable pace.

www.hitbtc.com/exchange/ETH-to-BTC

The Ethereum exchange website will give you the information you need into the Ethereum market, trends, and what to think about when speculating the price action of Ethereum, Bitcoin, or other altcoins.

www.bitfinex.com

This secure site allows you to create an account to exchange Ether and Bitcoin. The exchange can be something novel if you've never done currency speculation before and the website helps clear up any questions.

www.bitcoin.org

The most dedicated web site to everything Bitcoin.

www.coindesk.com/price

Latest prices of Bitcoin, Ether, and other CCs

www.coinmarketcap.com

Snapshot of the current market caps of CCs as well as available coins in all markets.

www.bankrate.com/finance/investing/cryptocurrency-alternatives-to-bitcoin-1.aspx

Comparing and contrasting Bitcoin to other CCs

Other resources and general knowledge:

www.investopedia.com

www.blockchain.info

And here are some of the exchange markets you can use to get Ether:

www.kraken.com

www.gatecoin.com

www.bittrex.com

www.poloniex.com

www.livecoin.net

www.bittylicious.com

www.metaexchange.info

www.bitfinex.com

www.c-cex.com

www.bleutrade.com

www.hitbtc.com

www.coinsquare.io

www.alcurex.org

www.yunbi.com

Other books, by Jeff Reed

- *Smart Contracts: The Essential Guide to Using Blockchain Smart Contracts for Cryptocurrency Exchange*
- *Blockchain: The Essential Guide to Understanding the Blockchain Revolution*
- *Fintech: Financial Technology and Modern Finance in the 21st Century*

Available on Kindle, audiobook and paperback form.

Check out Jeff Reed's other books on Amazon:

http://bit.ly/JeffReedBooks

www.ingramcontent.com/pod-product-compliance
Lightning Source LLC
Chambersburg PA
CBHW060414190526
45169CB00002B/895